HAIR DANCE!

WORDS BY
DINAH JOHNSON

PHOTOGRAPHS BY
KELLY JOHNSON

SQUARE
FISH

HENRY HOLT AND COMPANY • NEW YORK

For some special little sisters: Olania Washington, Angel Sledge, Malyka Norville, Evan Bowman, Jasmine Gordon, Bria McKenzie, Taja Geiger, Marley Thomson, Jaden Parker, Carlisle and Chandler Cooper, Jahnyah Francis, Nyah Taylor-Butcher, and, as always, for Taelor Johnson and Niani Feelings
—D. J.

In Memory of my grandparents, Benjamin and Mary Rose Dean, and the Dean's Beauty Salon and Barber Shop founders.
—K. J.

Thank you to my husband, Thiel Johnson, and my daughters, Natasha and Nicole Johnson. Thank you to my mother, Gloria Ella Dean-Tims, who shared her beauty and elegance with all. Thank you to Dinah Johnson and to Laura Godwin, Caroline Meckler, Laurent Linn, and the rest of the team at MCPG. Special thanks to Lillie and Monroe Jefferies, Nicole Johnson, Nyasha Bryant, Alexandra Rossi, Keyaira Rentie, Furaha-Esube, Regan Mims, Lavosha Baker, Zoie Sheng, Ashley Strader, Miranda Streeter, KaelinPierce, Mariah Jackson, Jacci Walker, Mariah and Marquiah Ladd, Nina Stewart, Jasmine Barber, Asasia Richardson, Madison Hairston, Marlicia McDonald, Sanari Robertson, and Aliyah Williams.

SQUARE FISH

An imprint of Macmillan Publishing Group, LLC
120 Broadway, New York, NY 10271 • mackids.com

Square Fish and the Square Fish logo are trademarks of Macmillan and are used by Henry Holt and Company under license from Macmillan.

Our books may be purchased in bulk for promotional, educational, or business use. Please contact your local bookseller or the Macmillan Corporate and Premium Sales Department at (800) 221-7945 ext. 5442 or by email at MacmillanSpecialMarkets@macmillan.com.

Library of Congress Cataloging-in-Publication Data
Johnson, Dinah.
Hair dance! / by Dinah Johnson; photographs by Kelly Johnson.—1st ed.
p. cm.
Includes bibliographical references.
ISBN-13: 978-0-8050-6523-7 / ISBN-10: 0-8050-6523-7
[1. Hair—Fiction.] I. Johnson, Kelly, ill. II. Title.
PS3560.O3747H35 2007   811'.54—dc22   2006030616
Originally published in the United States by Henry Holt and Company
First Square Fish edition, 2024
Book design and hand lettering by Laurent Linn

Square Fish logo designed by Filomena Tuosto
Printed in China by Toppan Leefung Printing Ltd., Dongguan City, Guangdong Province

ISBN 978-1-250-33171-7
10 9 8 7 6 5 4 3 2 1

PHOTOGRAPHER'S INTRODUCTION

My love of hair goes back to my grandparents, Benjamin and Mary Rose Dean, who dreamed of owning a successful business doing what they enjoyed: hairstyling. Though my grandparents are no longer with us, the salon they founded in 1954, Dean's Beauty Salon and Barber Shop, has remained in the family. My mother, Gloria Ella Dean-Tims, worked alongside her parents for many years, building a strong family and professional bond. The legacy of the salon was passed down to my mother's capable hands, and for the next fifty years, the salon thrived with grace and elegance. Dean's was successfully passed down to the next generation. It is now on the National Register of Historic Places, and is the oldest continuously operated Black-owned business in Oregon.

As a child, I worked at Dean's. I would take out rollers, clean combs and brushes, and get lunches for the staff and clients. In my spare moments, I watched as men, women, and children got "beautified" (as my grandmother always said), and I was in awe of the contribution my grandparents made to their family and community. A visit to the salon lifts the spirit and moves the soul. It creates energy—coolness, beauty, movement, and pride.

My pride in my grandparents' legacy was the inspiration for this book. Hair is our crowning glory, and every day we should appreciate its grace, color, and texture. I wanted to portray African-American hair in the most radiant light, as my mother and grandparents did.

The girls I photographed are the ones who truly give life to this book. Their innate gifts sparkle superbly, and I am grateful for the opportunity to have them as my radiant models. They embraced their individuality and exuded elegance. As readers delve into this book, my hope is for them to embark on a journey of self-discovery, acceptance, and self-confidence.

Hair Dance is a celebration of beauty, joy, diverse hairstyles, and self-love. I hope every young reader sees this book as a mirror of their beauty and empowerment, and it gives them permission to embrace their beautiful journey.

We play beauty parlor
every day
styling hair
in all kinds of ways

It's sassy short
and bouncy long
barrettes on my braids
keep the beat of the song

It's a wind song
a hair song

Camera's just about to click
strike a pose in red

showing off my Afro puffs

proud and pretty on my head

Braids swing with me
like water, moving free
no matter how I wear my hair
it's a special part of me

Special like my friends—
come on, you'll fit right in
with our rainbow tribe
of heritage
our sisterhood of hearts

People stare at my hair
sometimes—
it looks like
a work of art
and inside
I sing

It's a hair song

For my

Afro halo heavenly hair

My nature hair
real hair
flower power strong hair

Strong hair growing
into dreadlocks
(caring hands
make them love locs)

Mama's hands snap pictures
we can keep forever
of hair framing faces
full of friendship

Hats framing faces
full of happy

Heart happy
hair happy

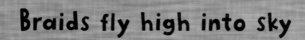

Braids fly high into sky

In a jump dance
street dance
friends dance
feet dance—

HAIR

DANCE!

Writer's Note

The girls and ladies in my life have hair that is every length, every color, every texture. We love our hair plain and pretty, or adorned with cowrie shells and hair jewelry. Hair—and how we care for it and for each other—is one of our most important links to the African heritages from which we descend. Our culture values beauty and improvisation in every realm of life, and hair is no exception. So we work with it, play with it, style it, and treasure it as the Art that it is.

—Dinah Johnson

To read more about hair and its history—in some ways it embodies the history of a whole people—look for these books:

For the little sisters
It's All Good Hair: The Guide to Styling and Grooming Black Children's Hair by Michele N-K. Collison (Amistad, 2002).
Kids Talk Hair: An Instruction Book for Grown-Ups and Kids by Pamela Ferrell (Cornrows and Company, 1999).
Kinki Kreations: A Parent's Guide to Natural Black Hair Care for Kids by Jena Renee Williams (Harlem Moon, 2004).
Wavy, Curly, Kinky: The African American Child's Hair Care Guide by Deborah R. Lilly (Wiley, 2005).

For the ladies
Bulletproof Diva: Tales of Race, Sex, and Hair by Lisa Jones (Anchor, 1997).
Hair Matters: Beauty, Power and Black Women's Consciousness by Ingrid Banks (New York University Press, 2000).
Hair Raising: Beauty, Culture, and African American Women by Noliwe M. Rooks (Rutgers University Press, 1996).
Hair Story: Untangling the Roots of Black Hair in America by Ayana D. Byrd and Lori L. Tharps (St. Martin's, 2002).
On Her Own Ground: The Life and Times of Madam C. J. Walker by A'Lelia Bundles (Scribner, 2002).
Tenderheaded: A Comb-Bending Collection of Hair Stories by Pamela Johnson and Juliette Harris
    (Washington Square Press, 2002).